Published by YOUniversal Center
Los Angeles, California

contact: info@youniversal.org

A YEAR OF LOVE

52 SHORT POEMS BY RUMI

translations

by

OMID ARABIAN

About This Book

The poems that follow are selections from *Divan-e Shams-e Tabrizi*, the collected poems of Jalaaleddin Mohammad Balkhi, known as Rumi (1207-1273 CE). Specifically, they are all in the form of Quatrain (*'Ruba'i'*) - a poem that consists of two lines, each line divided in half.

The source poem for each translation appears in the original Farsi language in calligraphic form at the top of each spread, and also at the end of the book along with a corresponding transliteration.

How To Use

Readers are invited to delve into this collection with an open heart, and treat Rumi's mystical poems as springboards for their own journeys of inquiry. One suggested approach is to reflect on each of the 52 poems for one week (hence the book's title), and use the blank facing pages to write down ruminations and revelations.

1

In the circle
of lovers
there's a peace
like no other;
for this wine
of love
there's a thirst
like no other;

there are
certain skills
to be learned
in school -
but love
is a skill
that is
like no other.

2

Love arrived,
and became
as blood in my veins,
beneath my skin...
until
it emptied me of me
and filled me
with the Beloved.

Every part of my being
was taken over
by the Beloved;
now,
my name
is all that's left of me -
everything else
is her.

3

All day
I praised you -
and I did not know!
All night
I lay with you -
and I did not know!

When I thought
of myself,
I thought I was me;
but I was you
through and through,
and I did not know!

4

When the ocean of All
becomes who I am
then I will see clearly
the beauty of each part.

I burn like a candle
on this path of love
so time can become
just one moment to me.

5

Mine
is a love
more pure
than clear water;
to be lost
in this love
is my right.

Others
have love
that wanes
and vascillates;
but my love
and Beloved
never fade.

6

Today
my hidden mate came forth
and pulled me by the hand;
today
I got so out of hand
I tore off all the chains.

Today
I am not just one drunk -
I am a hundred drunks;
today
I am a lunatic
who worships lunatics.

7

Wherever I touch
my head to the ground,
She's always the one
to whom I bow down;
in six directions,
and outside them all,
She's always the one
I worship and exalt.

Meadows and gardens,
flowers and trees,
nightingales, beauties,
and the whirling dance,
each is nothing but
a pretext, a guise!
She's always the one -
the point of it all.

8

My heart
speaks only
of your Spring;
my spirit
tells only tales
of your field of tulips;

it drinks
from your languid eyes,
so it can serve
your moist
ruby
lips.

9

From the fire
of your love,
a state of youth
rises up;
from your presence
in my heart,
murderous beauty
rises up.

If you are
to murder me,
then do it —
you're absolved!
From those who die
by your hand,
life itself
rises up.

10

All year long
may lovers be
scandalously drunk;
frenzied,
and delirious,
and insane with love.

In soberness,
we fret and grieve
for every little thing;
in drunkenness
we can allow
all that is to be.

11

There is a field
beyond heresy
and beyond piety -
it is there
in that space
that I wish to be.

Those who seek truth
lay down their head
when they arrive
in that field -
a place
where there is no piety,
and no heresy;
a place
that is not a place.

12

If you
are the sea
I'm a fish
in your water;
if you
are a meadow
I'm a deer
in your field.

So breathe
into me –
I'm a slave
to your breaths!
I am
your clarion,
your clarion,
your clarion.

13

Those
who have eyes
to see you,
my love,
how could
they ever look
at another
beloved?

To those
who have looked
towards you
my love,
sun and moon
appear
dim and dark,
I swear.

14

I hear
the wind bringing
a message from her;
I hear
the drunk nightingale
singing her name;

I hear
from her rooftop
a song that describes
an image I've seen
on the gates of my heart.

15

Once,
I was sober
and clever
like you;
once
I denied
all the lovers
in the world.

Now
I am drunk,
insane,
without a care;
now
it's as though
I have always
been this way.

16

Seek
the knowingness
that will untangle
your knots;
seek it
before
your spirit
leaves you.

Let go
that which is not,
but appears
to be;
and seek
that which is,
but appears
not to be.

17

This solitude
is worth
more than
a thousand lives;
this freedom
is worth
more than
all the world.

To be alone
with the divine
for a time
is worth
more than this,
more than that,
more than life,
more than the world.

18

There is
a path
from our heart
to our mouth;
a path
to the mysteries
of spirit
and the universe;

while the mouth
is closed,
that path
is open;
when the mouth
is opened,
that path
is closed.

19

Perhaps
you are clinging
too tightly
to this event;
nothing
will come
from striving
desperately.

A key
must arrive
by way
of Divine grace –
a key
to unlock
an event
such as this.

20

Listen
if you have
the power
of hearing:
to unite
with her
is to detach
from your self.

In the realm
of sight,
become silent
- make no sound -
because
she speaks
only
through visions.

21

Why do you become
weary and dull
when you enter
into silence?
Make silence your habit -
for silence
is the foundation,
the principle.

When you are in silence,
the one you call silent
will become
a hundred calls,
a hundred roars,
a hundred prophecies,
a hundred prophets.

22

I fade
into God
and so,
God is mine;
don't look
here and there -
She dwells
in my soul.

I am
my own ruler;
but so
you can't see,
I say
there's someone
who rules
over me.

23

Through love
of the Divine
you'll come
to no harm;
you won't
lose your life –
you'll become
life itself.

At the start,
you've come
from the sky
to the earth;
in the end,
you'll rise
from the earth
to the sky.

24

Outside
this world
is One
unknown to us;
outside
this life,
is One
who nurtures us;

I've made
her acquaintance
enough
to know this:
we are
her shadow
and this world
is ours.

25

I'll go
a hundred stations
beyond reason,
beyond mind;
I'll be
completely free -
from the constraints
of good and bad.

I am
so much virtue
behind the cover
of this veil;
I'll fall
(o heedless ones)
deeply in love
with my self.

26

Today
we are whirling,
whirling,
whirling;
pure light
is shining,
shining,
shining.

This love
is ruling.
ruling,
ruling;
reason
is leaving,
leaving,
leaving.

27

Don't fear
the events
that are born
of this world;
don't fear
what arrives -
it won't last
very long!

This life
is but a moment -
consider it
a gift;
don't ponder
what has gone,
and don't fear
what's to come.

28

O my heart,
hold on to hope
and don't despair;
o my heart,
countless wonders
are yet to come,
yet unseen.

If the whole world
conspires
to take your life,
o my heart,
do not let go
of the Beloved's
coattails.

29

You are
an edition
of the divine book;
you are
a mirror
reflecting
the King's beauty.

Whatever is in this world
is not outside of you;
whatever you desire,
seek it within yourself -
because you
are it.

30

Sometimes
we're hidden,
sometimes
in plain sight;
sometimes
a Muslim,
a Christian,
a Jew;

we will,
every day,
take on
a new form -
'til this
heart of ours
can hold
every heart.

31

You gaze
unto me
through the eyes
of denial –
for you
have not drunk
from that grand
cup of wine!

My joy
turns the world
into sweet
paradise;
sorrow
is my fool,
and the king
of others.

32

In this
world of mud
we are
hidden treasure;
we are
the possessors
of a land
beyond time.

Once
we pass through
the darkness
of mud,
we are
everliving,
and the fountain
of life.*

*Rumi refers specifically to the prophet Khidr, who is said to have
drunk water from the source of life and thus become immortal.

33

Today
there's someone
who's dancing
in this house,
someone
before whom
perfection
seems flawed.

And if
within you,
throbs a vein
of denial,
she'll shine
- like the moon -
on your denial
as well.

34

Though this life will pass
and come to an end,
our gift from Divine
is a far different life;
though this mortal life
is not here to stay,
there's life immortal
that will always remain.

Enter into love
- the water of life -
step into this water,
this ocean of love;
every single drop
is fully alive -
each drop in this ocean
is a life in itself.

35

Travel by night -
night will guide you
to the secrets,
hidden
from strangers' eyes.

The heart
is steeped in love,
the eyes
are steeped in dreams;
until morning arrives,
we are enthralled
with the Beloved's beauty.

36

On that day
when my spirit
heads for
the seventh sky,
and all parts
of my body
are claimed
by wretched soil,

come write
with your finger
upon the soil:
Arise!
Then I'll emerge
from the soil,
and my body
will come to life.

37

If you pursue
your base desires
and fleeting whims,
then you will go
in poverty -
an indigent.

And if you pass
beyond all this,
then you will see
as plain as day
why you have come
and where you'll go.

38

Tranquil
is the one
not gripped by
more or less;
not caught
in the binds
of poverty
or wealth;

set free
from the pains
of this world
and its masses;
not trapped
in the chasm
of kinship
with himself.

39

Oh where
is the moon
that's not above
nor below?
Oh where
is the spirit
that's not with us
nor without?

Don't say
here and there...
tell me the truth:
where is She?
She is
the whole world,
but who has eyes
that can see?

40

You,
who are singular
as the sun –
please come!
Without you
all nature
is pallid -
please come!

Without you
this world
is dust and grime
please come!
Without you –
this feast
is lifeless
please come!

41

From nothingness
our horse set out
and traveled forth with love;
our dark of night
lit by the glow
of constant union's wine.

Till nothingness
dawns once again,
our lips will not be dry -
by virtue of
the wine that's not
forbidden in our creed.

42

If you seek your self,
step out of yourself;
abandon the creek
and head for the river.

The weight of this world
you haul, like a cow!
Spin around and rise;
rise above this world.

43

Within my heart
everything
– inside and out –
is all her;
within my body
my veins,
my blood,
my life –
are all her.

How could
piety
and heresy
exist here?
There is
no being
that I resemble -
because my being
is all her.

44

In the heat
of love's fire
all that's cold
becomes warm;
in the glow
of love's light
even rocks
become soft.

Beloved,
be not cross
if lovers
cross the line;
when we're drunk
on love's wine
inhibitions
become lost.

45

O love
you've never slept
and never will;
o love
you won't be seen
by those who sleep.

O love,
there's more to say
but I won't speak -
you, too,
have never said,
and never will.

46

Know this:
a lover cannot be
religious, or devout;
the creed of love
cannot contain
belief or blaspshemy.

In love,
there is
no mind, no heart,
no body, and no soul –
and anyone
who's not this way,
is truly not in love.

47

O wandering heart,
there is a path
through spirit
to the Beloved;
o lost one,
there is path
hidden
and evident.

If all six directions
are blocked,
fear not –
for there is a path
from the depth
of your being
towards
the Beloved.

48

Ever since
I heard
the tale of love
for the first time,
I've worn out my eyes
my heart
and my soul
along its path.

Lover
and Beloved –
are they two,
I asked?
No, it was me
whose eyes were crossed
and saw two
where there was one.

MONDAY

JANUARY
16

What do you call a magical dog?

A Labracadabrador.

• Martin Luther King Jr. Day (US)

49

She is
a secret garden:
hidden flowers,
invisible trees;
she is
a singular self
that appears
in a hundred forms;

she is
an ocean
that engulfs
all that is;
her every wave
gives rise
to a hundred more
in a hundred souls.

50

If I
pass away,
carry me
if you will;
entrust
my remains
to my love
if you will;

if she
gives a kiss
unto my
withered lips,
do not
be surprised
if I come
back to life.

51

Now
I've come to know
that Love's always with me
and I hold
in my hand
the thousand strands
of her hair;

though once
I was drunk
by virtue of the wine-cup,
now
the cup is drunk
by virtue
of me.

52

My essence
and yours
have always
been one;
my hidden self
and yours,
my evident self
and yours;

it's folly
to speak
of 'mine'
and of 'yours'...
now that
'you' and 'I'
are gone
from our midst.

Originals & Transliterations

In the pages that follow you will find Rumi's original Farsi poems, which correspond by number to the preceding translations.

For those who do not read Farsi but wish to hear what the original verses sound like, there is also a transliteration of each poem underneath each original. A key to the transliterations is below.

farsi letter/sound	transliteration	as in (english word)
اَ	a	cat
آ	aa	car
اُ	o	for
او	oo	boot
اِ	e	bed
ی	ee	sleep
ی	i	big
چ	ch	chalk
خ	kh	khutzpah
ژ	zh	measure
ق / غ	qh	qanat
گ	g	good

In addition, a capital H is used to denote a hard 'h' sound in the middle or at the end of a word, as in the word *mohair*.

در مجلس عشاق قراری دگر است
وین باده‌ی عشق را خماری دگر است

آن علم که در مدرسه حاصل کردند
کار دگر است و عشق کاری دگر است

———————— 1 ————————

Dar majles-e oshaaqh qharaari degar ast
Vin baadeh-ye eshqh raa khomaari degar ast

Aan elm keh dar madreseh haasel kardand
Kaar-e degar ast-o eshqh kaari degar ast

عشق آمد و شد چو خونم اندر رگ و پوست
تا کرد مرا تهی و پر کرد ز دوست

اجزای وجود من همه دوست گرفت
نامیست ز من بر من و باقی همه اوست

———————— 2 ————————

Eshqh aamad-o shod cho khoonam andar rag-o poost
Taa kard maraa tohi-yo por kard ze-doost

Ajzaa-ye vojood-e man hameh doost gereft
Naameest ze-man bar man-o baaqhi hameh oost

روزت بستودم و نمیدانستم
شب با تو غنودم و نمیدانستم

ظنّ برده بدم به‌خود که من من بودم
من جمله تو بودم و نمیدانستم

———————— 3 ————————

Roozat besotoodam-o nemidaanestam
Shab baa to qhonoodam-o nemidaanestam

Zan bordeh bodam beh-khod keh man man boodam
Man jomleh to boodam-o nemidaanestam

آن وقت که بحر کل شود ذات مرا
روشن گردد جمال ذرات مرا

زان می‌سوزم چو شمع تا در ره عشق
یك وقت شود جمله اوقات مرا

———————— 4 ————————

Aaan vaqht keh baHr-e kol shavad zaat maraa
Rowshan gardad jamaal-e zarraat maraa

Zaan meesoozam cho sham'e taa dar raH-e eshqh
Yek vaqht shavad jomleh-ye owqhaat maraa

عشقی دارم پاکتر از آب زلال
این باختن عشق مرا هست حلال

عشق دگران بگردد از حال به حال
عشق من و معشوق مرا نیست زوال

— 5 —

Eshqhi daaram paaktar az aab-e zolaal
In baakhtan-e eshqh maraa hast halaal

Eshqh-e degaraan begardad az haal beh haal
Eshqh-e man-o ma'shooqh-e maraa neest zavaal

آن یار نهان کشید دستم امروز
از دست شدم بند گسستم امروز

یك مست نیم هزار مستم امروز
دیوانه‌ی دیوانه پرستم امروز

— 6 —

Aan yaar-e naHaan kesheed dastam emrooz
Az dast shodam band gosastam emrooz

Yek mast niyam, hezaar mastam emrooz
Deevaneh-ye deevaaneh-parastam emrooz

بر هر جائی که سرنهم مسجود او است
در شش جهت و برون شش معبود اوست

باغ و گل و بلبل و سماع و شاهد
این جمله بهانه و همه مقصود اوست

— 7 —

Bar har jaa-yee keh sar-naham masjood oost
Dar shesh jeHat-o boroon-e shesh ma'bood oost

Baaqh-o gol-o bolbol-o samaa'o shaahed
Een jomleh bahaaneh-vo hameh maqhsood oost

دل جمله حکایت از بهار تو کند
جان جمله حدیث لاله‌زار تو کند

مستی ز دو چشم پرخمار تو کند
تا خدمت لعل آبدار تو کند

— 8 —

Del jomleh hekaayat az baHaar-e to konad
Jaan jomleh hadees-e laalehzaar-e to konad

Mastee ze-do chashm-e por-khomaar-e to konad
Taa khedmat-e la'al-e aaabdaar-e to konad

از آتش عشق تو جوانی خیزد
در سینه جمالهای جانی خیزد

گر می‌کشیم بکش حلالست ترا
کز کشته‌ی دوست زندگانی خیزد

--- 9 ---

Az aatash-e eshqh-e to javaanee kheezad
Dar seeneh jamaal-haa-ye jaanee kheezad

Gar meekoshiyam bekosh, halaalast toraa
Kaz koshteh-ye doost, zendegaanee kheezad

عاشق همه سال مست و رسوا بادا
دیوانه و شوریده و شیدا بادا

با هشیاری غصه‌ی هرچیز خوریم
چون مست شویم هرچه بادا بادا

--- 10 ---

Aasheqh hameh saal mast-o rosvaa baadaa
Deevaaneh-vo shooreedeh-vo sheydaa baadaa

Baa hoshyaari qhosseh-ye har cheez khoreem
Chon mast shaveem, harcheh baadaa baadaa

از کفر و ز اسلام برون صحرائیست

ما را به میان آن فضا سودائیست

عارف چو بدان رسید سر را بنهد

نه کفر و نه اسلام و نه آنجا جائیست

---------- 11 ----------

Az kofr-o ze-eslaam boron saHraa'iist
Maa raa beh-miyaan-e aan fazaa sodaa'iist

Aaref cho bedaan reseed, sar raa benehad
Na kofr-o na eslaam-o na anjaa jaa'iist

گر دریایی ماهی دریای تو ام

ور صحرایی آهوی صحرای تو ام

در من میدم بندهی دمهای تو ام

سرنای تو سرنای تو سرنای تو ام

---------- 12 ----------

Gar daryaayi maahi-ye daryaa-ye to-am
Var sahraayi aahoo-ye sahraa-ye to-am

Dar man meedam bandeh-ye damhaa-ye to-am
Sornaa-ye to sornaa-ye to sornaa-ye to-am

آن کس که ترا دیده بود ای دلبر
او چون نگرد بسوی معشوق دگر

در دیده هر آنکه کرد سوی تو نظر
تاریک نماید به خدا شمس و قمر

13

Man maHv-e khodaayam-o khodaa aan-e manast
Har soosh majoo'eed, keh dar jaan-e manast

Soltaan manam-o qhalat namaayam beh shomaa
Gooyam keh kasi hast keh soltaan-e manast

از باد همه پیام او میشنوم
و ز بلبل مست نام او میشنوم

این نقش عجب که دیدهام بر در دل
آوازهی آن ز بام او میشنوم

14

Az baad hameh payaam-e oo meeshanavam
Vaz bolbol-e mast, naam-e oo meeshanavam

In naqhsh-e ajab keh deedeh-am bar dar-e del
Aavaazeh-ye aan ze-baam-e oo meeshanavam

من نیز چو تو عاقل و هشیار بدم
بر جمله‌ی عاشقان به انکار بدم

دیوانه و مست و لاابالی گشتم
گوئی که همه عمر در این کار بدم

--- 15 ---

Man neez cho to aaqhel-o hoshyaar bodam
Bar jomleh-ye aaqheqhaan beh enkaar bodam

Deevaneh-vo mast-o laa-ebaalee gashtam
Goo'ii keh hameh omr dar in kaar bodam

علمی که ترا گره گشاید بطلب
زان پیش که از تو جان برآید بطلب

آن نیست که هست مینماید بگذار
آن هست که نیست مینماید بطلب

--- 16 ---

Elmee keh toraa gereH goshaayad betalab
Zaan peesh keh az to jaan bar-aayad betalab

Aan neest keh hast minemaayad begozaar
Aan hast keh neest minemaayad betalab

این تنهایی هزار جان بیش ارزد
این آزادی ملک جهان بیش ارزد

در خلوت یک زمانه با حق بودن
از جان و جهان و این و آن بیش ارزد

—— 17 ——

In tanhaayi hezaar jaan beesh arzad
In aazaadi molk-e jahaan beesh arzad

Dar khalvat yek zamaaneh baa haqh boodan
Az jaan-o jahaan-o een-o aan beesh arzad

راهی ز زبان ما بدل پیوسته است
کاسرار جهان و جان در او پیوسته است

تا هست زبان بسته گشاده است آن راه
چون گشت زبان گشاده آنره بسته است

—— 18 ——

Raahi ze-zabaan-e maa beh-del peyvast-ast
K'asraar-e jahaan-o jaan dar-oo peyvast-ast

Taa hast zabaan basteh, goshaad-ast aan raaH
Chon gasht zabaan goshaadeh, aanraH bast-ast

این واقعه را سخت بگیری شاید
از کوشش عاجزانه کاری ناید

از رحمت ایزدی کلیدی باید
تا قفل چنین واقعه را بگشاید

--------------------- 19 ---------------------

In vaaqhe'eh raa sakht begeeree shaayad
Az kooshesh-e aajezaaneh kaaree naayad

Az raHmat-e eezadee keleedee baayad
Ta qhofl'e chonin vaaghe'eh raa bogshaayad

بشنو اگرت تاب شنیدن باشد
پیوستن او ز خود بریدن باشد

خاموش کن آنجا که جهان نظر است
چون گفتن ایشان همه دیدن باشد

--------------------- 20 ---------------------

Beshnow agarat taab-e sheneedan baashad
Peyvastan-e oo ze-khod boreedan baashad

Khaamoosh kon aanjaa keh jahaan-e nazar ast
Chon goftan-e eeshaan hameh deedan baashad

در خاموشی چرا شوی کند و ملول
خو کن به خموشی که اصولست اصول

خود کو خمشی آنکه خمش میخوانی
صد بانگ و غریو است و پیامست و رسول

Dar khaamooshi cheraa shavi kond-o malool?
Khoo kon beh khamooshi keh osoolast, osool

Khod koo khamoshi aankeh khamosh mikhaani
Sad baang-o qhareevast-o payaamast-o rasool

من محو خدایم و خدا آن منست
هر سوش مجوئید که در جان منست

سلطان منم و غلط نمایم بشما
گویم که کسی هست که سلطان منست

22

Man maHv-e khodaayam-o khodaa aan-e manast
Har soosh majoo'eed, keh dar jaan-e manast

Soltaan manam-o qhalat namaayam beh shomaa
Gooyam keh kasi hast keh soltaan-e manast

از عشق خدا نه بر زیان خواهی شد
بی‌جان ز کجا شوی که جان خواهی شد

اول به زمین از آسمان آمده‌ای
آخر ز زمین بر آسمان خواهی شد

———— 23 ————

Az eshqh-e khodaa na bar ziyaan khaahee shod
Bee-jaan ze-kojaa shavee keh jaan khaahee shod

Avval beh-zamin az aasemaan aamadeh-ii
Aakher ze-zamin bar aasemaan khaahi shod

بیرون ز جهان و جان یکی دایه‌ی ماست
دانستن او نه درخور پایه‌ی ماست

در معرفتش همین قدر میدانم
ما سایه اوئیم و جهان سایه ماست

———— 24 ————

Beeroon ze-jahaan-o jaan yeki daayeh-ye maast
Daanestan-e oo na dar khor-e paayeh-ye maast

Dar ma'refatash hamin qhadar meedaanam
Maa saayeh-ye oo'eem-o jahaan saayeh-ye maast

صد مرحله زانسوی خرد خواهم شد

فارغ ز وجود نیك و بد خواهم شد

از بس خوبی كه در پس پرده منم

ای بیخبران عاشق خود خواهم شد

—————— 25 ——————

Sad marHaleh z'aansoo-ye kherad khaaham shod
Faareqh ze-vojood-e neek-o bad khaaham shod

Az bas khoobi keh dar pas-e pardeh manam
Ey bee-khabaraan aasheqh-e khod khaaham shod

امروز سماعست و سماعست و سماع

نورست شعاعست و شعاعست و شعاع

این عشق مطاعست و مطاعست و مطاع

از عقل وداعست و وداعست و وداع

—————— 26 ——————

Emrooz samaa'ast-o samaa'ast-o samaa'
Noorast sho'aa'ast-o sho'aa'ast-o sho'aa'

In eshqh mataa'ast-o mataa'ast-o mataa'
Az aqhl vedaa'ast-o vedaa'ast-o vedaa'

از حادثه‌ی جهان زاینده مترس
و ز هرچه رسد چو نیست پاینده مترس

این یکدم عمر را غنیمت میدان
از رفته میندیش و ز آینده مترس

27

Az haadeseh-ye jahaan-e zaayandeh matars
Vaz har-che resad cho neest paayandeh matars

In yek-dam-e omr raa qhanimat meedaan
Az rafteh mayandeesh-o ze aayandeh matars

نومید مشو امید میدارای دل
در غیب عجایب است بسیارای دل

گر جمله جهان قصد بجان تو کند
تو دامن دوست را نه بگذارای دل

28

No-meed mashow omeed meedaar ey del
Dar qheyb ajaayeb-ast besyaar ey del

Gar jomleh jahaan qhasd beh-jaan-e to konad
To daaman-e doost raa na-bogzaar ey del

ای نسخه‌ی نامه‌ی الهی که توئی
وی آینه‌ی جمال شاهی که توئی

بیرون ز تو نیست هرچه در عالم هست
در خود بطلب هر آنچه خواهی که توئی

— 29 —

Ey noskheh-ye naameh-ye elaahi keh toyi
Vey aayeneh-ye jamaal-e shaahi keh toyi

Biroon ze-to neest har cheh dar aalam hast
Dar khod betalab har-aancheh khaahi keh toyi

مائیم که گه نهان و گه پیدائیم
گه مومن و گه یهود و گه ترسائیم

تا این دل ما قالب هر دل گردد
هر روز به صورتی برون می‌آئیم

— 30 —

Maa'eem keh gaH nahaan-o gaH peydaa'iim
GaH mo'men-o gaH yahood-o gaH tarsaa'iim

Taa in del-e maa qhaaleb-e har del gardad
Har rooz beh-soorati boroon mi'aa'iim

ای یار به انکار سوی ما نگران
زیرا که نَخورده‌ای از آن رطل گران

از شادی من بهشت گردیده جهان
غم مسخرهی من است و میر دگران

31

Ey yaar-e beh-enkaar soo-ye maa negaraan
Zeera keh nakhordeh-ii az aan ratl-e geraan

Az shaadi-ye man beHesht gardideh jahaan
Qham maskhareh-ye man-ast-o meer-e degaraan

در عالم گل گنج نهانی ماییم
دارندهی ملک جاودانی ماییم

چون از ظلمات آب و گل بگذشتیم
هم خضرو هم آب زندگانی ماییم

32

Dar aalam-e gel ganj-e nahaani maayeem
Daarandeh-ye molk-e jaavedaani maayeem

Choon az zolamaat aab-o gel bogzashteem
Ham khezr-o ham aab-e zendegaani maayeem

امروز در این خانه کسی رقصانست
که کل کمال پیش او نقصانست

ور در تو ز انکار رگی جنبانست
آن ماه در انکار تو هم تابانست

33

Emrooz dar in khaaneh kasi raqhsaan-ast
Keh koll-e kamaal, peesh-e oo naqhsaan-ast

Var dar to ze-enkaar ragi jonbaan-ast
Aan maaH dar enkaar-e to ham taabaan-ast

گر عمر بشد عمر دگر داد خدا
گر عمر فنا نماند نک عمر بقا

عشق آب حیاتست در این آب درآ
هر قطره از این بحر حیاتست جدا

34

Gar omr beshod omr-e degar daad khodaa
Gar omr-e fanaa namaand, nak omr-e baqhaa

Eshqh aab-e hayaat-ast, dar-in aab dar-aa
Har qhatreh az-in baHr, hayaatast jodaa

شب رو که شبت راهبر اسرار است
زیرا که نهان ز دیده‌ی اغیار است

دل عشق‌آلود و دیده‌ها خواب‌آلود
تا صبح جمال یار ما را کار است

---- 35 ----

Shab row keh shabat raaHbar-e asraarast
Zeera keh nahaan ze deedeh-ye aqhyaarast

Del eshqh-alood-o deedeh-haa khaab-aalood
Taa sobH jamaal-e yaar maa raa kaarast

آن روز که جانم ره کیوان گیرد
اجزای تنم خاک پریشان گیرد

بر خاک بانگشت تو بنویس که خیز
تا بر‌جهم از خاک و تنم جان گیرد

---- 36 ----

Aan rooz keh jaanam raH-e keyvaan geerad
Ajzaa-ye tanam khaat-e pareeshaan geerad

Bar khaak beh-angosht to benvees keh kheez
Taa bar-jaham az khaak-o tanam jaan geerad oost

گر بر سر شهوت و هوا خواهی رفت
از من خبرت که بینوا خواهی رفت

ور درگذری از این ببینی به عیان
کز بهر چه آمدی کجا خواهی رفت

Gar bar sar-e shaHvat-o havaa khaahi raft
Az man khabarat keh beenavaa khaahi raft

Var dar-gozari az in, bebini beh-ayaan
Kaz baHr-e cheh aamadi, kojaa khaahi raft

آسوده کسی که در کم و بیشی نیست
در بند توانگری و درویشی نیست

فارغ ز غم جهان و از خلق جهان
با خویشتنش بدرهی خویشی نیست

Aasoodeh kasi keh dar kam-o beeshee neest
Dar band-e tavangaree-yo darveeshee neest

Faareqh ze-qham-e jahaan-o az khalqh-e jahaan
Baa kheeshtanash beh-darreh-ye kheeshee neest

ماهی که نه زیر و نی به بالاست کجاست
جانی که نه بی‌ما و نه با ماست کجاست

اینجا آنجا مگو بگو راست کجاست
عالم همه اوست آنکه بیناست کجاست

—— 39 ——

Maahi keh na zeer-o ney beh baalaast kojaast?
Jaani keh na bee maa vo na baa maast kojaast?

Injaa aanjaa magoo, begoo raast kojaast?
Aaalam hameh oost, aankeh beenaast kojaast?

ای آنکه چو آفتاب فرد است بیا
بیرون تو برگ و باغ زرد است بیا

عالم بی‌تو غبار و گرد است بیا
این مجلس عیش بی‌تو سرد است بیا

—— 40 ——

Ey aankeh cho aaftaab fard-ast, biyaa
Beeroon-e to barg-o baaqh zard-ast, biyaa

Aaalam bee to qhobaar-o gard-ast, biyaa
In majless-e eysh bee-to sard-ast, biyaa

با عشق روان شد از عدم مرکب ما
روشن ز شراب وصل دائم شب ما

زان می که حرام نیست در مذهب ما
تا صبح عدم خشک نیابی لب ما

Baa eshqh ravaan shod az adam markab-e maa
Rowshan ze-sharaab-e vasl-e daa'em shab-e maa

Zaan mey keh haraam neest dar mazHab-e maa
Taa sobH-e adam khoshk nayaabee lab-e maa

گر در طلب خودی ز خود بیرون آ
جو را بگذار و جانب جیحون آ

چون گاو چه میکشی تو بار گردون
چرخی بزن و بر سر این گردون آ

Gar dar talab-e khodee ze-khod beeroon-aa
Joo raa begozaar-o jaaneb-e jeyhoon-aa

Chon gaav cheh mikeshi to baar-e gardoon?
Charkhi bezan-o bar sar-e in gardoon aa

اندر دل من درون و بیرون همه او است
اندر تن من جان و رگ و خون همه اوست

اینجای چگونه کفر و ایمان گنجد
بی‌چون باشد وجود من چون همه اوست

— 43 —

Andar del-e man daroon-o beeroon hameh oost
Andar tan-e man jaan-o rag-o khoon hameh oost

Injaay chegooneh kofr-o eemaan gonjad
Bee-choon baashad vojood-e man chon hameh oost

از آتش عشق سردها گرم شود
وز تابش عشق سنگها نرم شو

ای دوست گناه عاشقان سخت مگیر
کز باده‌ی عشق مرد بی‌شرم شود

— 44 —

Az aatash-e eshqh sard-haa garm shavvad
Vaz taabesh-e eshqh sang-haa narm shavad

Ey doost, gonaaH-e aasheqhaan sakht mageer
Kaz baadeh-ye eshqh mard bee-sharm shavad

ای عشق نخسبی و نخفتی هرگز
در دیده‌ی خفتگان نیفتی هرگز

باقی سخنی هست نگویم او را
تو نیز نگوئی و نگفتی هرگز

--- 45 ---

Ey eshqh nakhosbi-yo nakhofti hargez
Dar deedeh-ye khoftegaan nayoftee hargez

Baaqhee sokhani hast, nagooyam oo ra
To neez nagooyee-yo nagofti hargez

عاشق تو یقین دان که مسلمان نبود
در مذهب عشق کفر و ایمان نبود

در عشق تن و عقل و دل و جان نبود
هرکس که چنین نگشت او آن نبود

--- 46 ---

Aasheqh to yaqhin daan keh mosalmaan nabovad
Dar mazHab-e eshqh, kofr-o eemaan anbovad

Dar eshqh tan-o aqhl-o del-o jaan nabovad
Har kass keh chonin nagasht, oo aan nabovad

سرگشته دلا به دوست از جان راهست
ای گمشده آشکار و پنهان راهست

گر شش جهتت بسته شود باك مدار
کز قعر نهادت سوی جانان راهست

—— 47 ——

Sargashteh delaa beh doost az jaan raaHast
Ey gomshodeh aashkaar-o penhaan raaHast

Gar shesh jehatat basteh shavad baak madaar
Kaz qha'ar-e nahaadat soo-ye jaanan raaHast

زاول که حدیث عاشقی بشنودم
جان و دل و دیده در رهش فرسودم

گفتم که مگر عاشق و معشوق دو اند
خود هر دو یکی بود من احول بودم

—— 48 ——

Z'avval keh haees-e aasheqhi beshnoodam
Jaan-o del-o deedeh dar raHash farsoodam

Goftam keh magar aasheqh-o ma'shooqh do-and
Khod har-do yeki bood, man aHval boodam

گلباغ نهانست و درختان پنهان

صد سان بنماید او و او خود یکسان

بحریست محیط و بی‌حد و بی‌پایان

صد موج ز موج او درون صد جان

――――――― 49 ―――――――

Golbaaqh-e nahaanast-o derakhtaan penhaan
Sad saan benamaayd oo vo oo khod yeksaan

BaHreest moheet-o bee-had-o bee-paayaan
Sad mowj ze-mowj-oo daroon-e sad jaan

گر من میرم مرا بیارید شما

مرده به نگار من سپارید شما

گر بوسه دهد بر لب پوسیده‌ی من

گر زنده شوم عجب مدارید شما

――――――― 50 ―――――――

Gar man meeram maraa biyaareed shomaa
Mordeh beh negaar-e man sepaareed maraa

Gar booseh dehad bar lab-e pooseedeh-ye man
Gar zendeh shavam ajab madaareed maraa

چون دانستم که عشق پیوست منست

وان زلف هزار شاخ در دست منست

هرچند که دی مست قدح میبودم

امروز چنانم که قدح مست منست

Chon daanestam keh eshqh peyvast-e manast
Vaan zolf-e hezaar-shaakh dar dast-e manast

Har chand keh di mast-e qhadaH miboodam
Emrooz chonaanam keh qhadaH mast-e manast oost

در اصل یکی بدست جان من و تو

پیدای من و تو و نهان من و تو

خامی باشد که گویی آن من و تو

برخاست من و تو از میان من و تو

Dar asl yeki bodast jaan-e man-o to
Peydaa-ye man-o to-vo nahaan-e man-o to

Khaami baashad keh gooyi aan-e man-o to
Barkhaast man-o to az miyaan-e man-o to

Translator's Note - In Gratitude

First and foremost, I offer gratitude to the spirit of Rumi, and to A.M.S. for opening my heart's eyes to this magnificent spirit.

This is the third collection of translations to come out of a course I have conducted since 2010, and so I am grateful to all who have attended and/or supported the course and made this volume possible.

I am overjoyed about the sublime work of art that graces the cover of this book; I thank the artist Sheila Karbassian for creating it, and the owner of the work (Mr. Christopher Judge) for his kind permission.

While any act of translation inherently involves some degree of subjective interpretation, I have striven to keep as much as possible to the letter of Rumi's verses and not just to their spirit. I thank Kouross Esmaeli for his astute suggestions on the translations as they evolved.

Always and forever I am indebted to Mojdeh for far more than can be enumerated here.

Last but by no means least, I offer gratitude to you, the reader, for taking this journey into love, with Rumi as your guide.

O.A.

ALSO AVAILABLE:

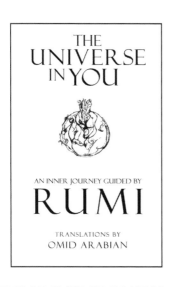

THE UNIVERSE IN YOU
Thirty-four new translations
of Rumi, along with
the original poems
and beautiful illustrations.
ISBN 9780692434451

DANCING INTO THE LIGHT
Thirty-seven new translations
of Rumi, along with
the original poems
and beautiful illustrations.
ISBN 9780692434451

THE HEART'S GARDEN
Based on a poem by Rumi.
This fully illustrated story-
book empowers kids an
adults by reminding them
of their inter-connectednes
to all and their ability
to transform the world.
Winner of the 2015
Gelett Burgess Award.
ISBN 9780692514801

Made in the USA
Middletown, DE
26 December 2022